Making
Dolls' Clothes

Making Dolls' Clothes

Diana Walker

Illustrated by
Diana and Roger Walker

B T Batsford Ltd *London*

For Suzy

First published 1980

ISBN 0 7134 3319 1

Printed in Great Britain by
The Garden City Press, Letchworth, Herts
for the publishers B T Batsford Ltd
4 Fitzhardinge Street, London W1H 0AH

Contents

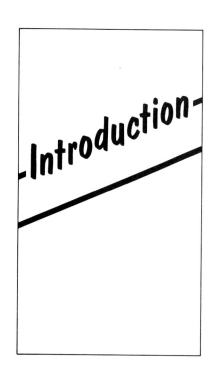

Introduction

Commercially made dolls' clothes are very expensive and in general poorly made. Seams tend to come undone and the fastenings fall off after a short time. This is not only disappointing, but frustrating to the young owners.

Here is a chance for those with a basic knowledge of sewing to put their skills to a use which will give children hours of enjoyment.

There are, of course, those, who once started on the work will prefer to branch off on their own, making their dolls' clothes to suit their own individual tastes. These people have been catered for by providing ideas for variations on each pattern including many accessories.

Try out new methods, so original ways of working of your own will emerge: be it a Red-Indian's costume decorated with beads and fabric paint or a simple lace-edged smock.

Basic measuring ensures that the garment or accessories fit the doll for which they are made. Dolls vary enormously from chubby to slim, short to tall and traditionally child-shaped to fashionably elongated. Once the basic measurements have been made the techniques used to assemble the clothes are common to any shape of doll.

Pins — Glass-headed pins are the easiest to use as they are sharper than ordinary pins. They are also less likely to get lost in the work.

Sewing threads — Mercerdised cotton, for sewing cotton fabrics
Polyster thread, for sewing synthetic fabrics
Buttonhole thread for sewing leather and suede
Embroidery silk for sewing appliqué, embroidery stitches and shoelaces.

Scissors — A pair of very sharp scissors for cutting fabric
A pair of scissors for cutting paper
A pair of small pointed scissors for cutting loose ends of cotton and unpicking short seams
A pair of pinking shears for neatening seams

Needles — A varied range of needles to allow for the different types of fabric likely to be used. The finer the fabric, the finer the needle.
A large-eyed needle for the threading of elastic
A glover's needle for sewing leather and suede

Measuring equipment —
A cloth tape-measure
A ruler
A pair of compasses

Other supplies
A thimble
An ironing board and iron
A pressing-cloth (an old pillow-case or tea towel is ideal)
An orange stick for pushing out corners on collars etc to a point
Stiff paper for making patterns
Adhesive (rubber-solution glue)

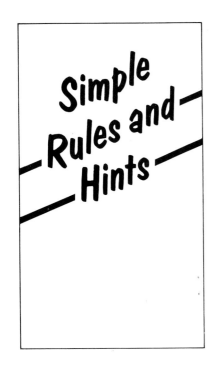

Simple Rules and Hints

Wash your hands before you begin.

Work in a good light.

Keep your work-surface clean.

Keep all work in progress in a cloth bag when not being sewn.

Keep fitting the garment onto the doll as you work.

Press each seam as you work.

Neaten all seams.

Fasten-off all sewing securely.

Remove all pins from finished sewing.

Keep all pins in a box or a pincushion. (If a few grains of rice are kept in the box or in the centre of the pincushion the pins will not rust.)

Do not keep pins in the same box as needles.

Keep pointed scissors stuck in a cork

When cutting-out use long smooth cutting strokes.

When cutting curves, turn the fabric into the scissors and not the scissors into the fabric.

Never sew with a thread longer than the distance from the tip of your fingers to your elbow.

Avoid using a knot wherever possible. (It is much better to take a couple of tiny back-stitches than to have a stress point where the knot occurs.)

Always thread the needle with the newly cut end of the thread.

Do not use widely different weights of fabric in the same garment. If this cannot be avoided, back the lighter fabric with an interlining.

Always place the pattern pieces with the straight grain of the fabric running from the top to bottom unless otherwise stated.

Sew press-studs on as firmly as possible.

Stitch around armhole seams twice.

Before you begin to make any garment read the instructions all the way through and study the working diagrams.

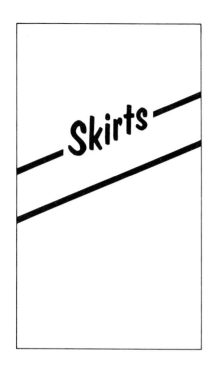

THE SIMPLE GATHERED SKIRT

Measuring
Width of material needed
Using figure A as a guide, measure around the doll's waist.

Write this measurement down. Add the same amount again and 2 cm (¾ in.) for the seam allowances.

For example: If the doll's waist measures 20 cm (8 in.) add a further 20 cm (8 in.) and the 2 cm (¾ in.) seam allowance.

Thus 20 cm + 20 cm + 2 cm = 42 cm
(8 in. + 8 in. + ¾ in. = 16¾ in.).

This is the width of material needed.

Depth of material needed
Measure from the doll's waist to where you decide the finished lower edge of the skirt should be.

Add 3 cm (1¼ in.) for the cased turning.

Add 3 cm (1¼ in.) for the hem.

A

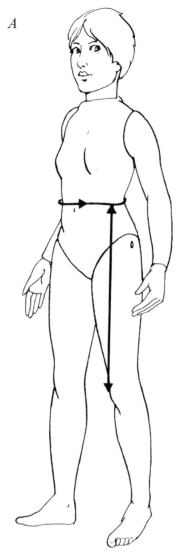

For example: if you decide the finished depth of the skirt will be 8 cm (3¼ in.) add a further 6 cm (2½ in.) for the turnings

Thus 8 cm + 3 cm + 3 cm = 14 cm
(3¼ in. + 1¼ in. + 1¼ in. = 5¾ in.)

This is the depth of material needed.

Materials needed
Estimated length of cotton fabric
Sewing cotton to match

A length of 5 mm (¼ in.) elastic for the doll's waist
Lace or broderie anglaise to fit around the lower edge of the skirt
A bodkin
Rubber-solution glue (optional).

Making the skirt
Using the calculated measurements, cut out the skirt.
With right sides together fold the fabric in half and seam up the short sides (figure 1).

1

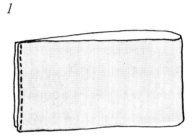

Fasten off the seam securely. Turn the top edge over (right side to wrong side) to make the casing for the elastic. Sew into place leaving 2 cm (¾ in.) open for the threading of the elastic.

Turn up the hem and glue or sew it into place (figure 2).

2

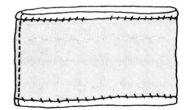

Using a large bodkin thread the elastic into the top hem and stitch the ends of the elastic together firmly (figure 3).

3

Leave the 2 cm (¾ in.) opening open so that new elastic can be inserted if necessary. Children are rather rough on elastic and the elastic may go before the skirt wears out.

Sew or glue broderie Anglaise to the inside of the hem so that it shows below the edge of the skirt (figure 4).

4

SKIRT WITH WAISTBAND

Measuring
Length of material needed, plus the waistband
Measure as for the simple gathered skirt on page 9.
Waistband
Measure the doll's waist
Add 2 cm (¾ in.) for the seam allowances and 1 cm (⅜ in.) for the overlap of the waistband fastening.

For example: if the doll's waist measures 20 cm (8 in.) add a further 1 cm (⅜ in.) for the overlap and 2 cm (¾ in.) for the seam allowances.
This gives you a total of 23 cm (9⅛ in.)
This is the length of material needed.
Depth of material needed
Decide on the depth of the finished waistband and double this measurement.
Add 2 cm (¾ in.) to this measurement for the seam allowances.
This is the depth of material needed.

Materials needed
Estimated length of cotton fabric
Sewing cotton to match
A press-stud
Rubber-solution glue (optional)

Making the skirt
With right sides together fold the fabric for the skirt in half and sew halfway up the short sides.
Fasten off the seam securely.
Run a gathering thread along the top edge of the skirt (figure 5).

5

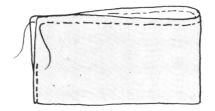

Press under the seam allowance from the right side to the wrong side along one long edge and the two ends of the waistband (figure 6).

6

Pull up the gathering thread on the skirt so that the gathered fabric fits the waistband less 1 cm (⅜ in.) for the waistband fastening.
With right sides together, pin the unpressed edge of the waistband over the gathered edge of the skirt with 1 cm (⅜ in.) extending over one end for the back fastening (figure 7).

7

Sew the skirt to the waistband.
Turn the waistband over the top edge of the skirt and slip stitch it to the inside of the skirt (figure 8).

8

Sew a press-stud onto the waistband using buttonhole stitch (figure 9).
Turn up the hem and sew or glue it into place.

9

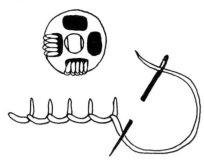

DECORATING A PLAIN SKIRT

A plain skirt can be easily brightened by adding trimmings.
Decorations are much more effective if kept simple and used in moderation.
The following ideas are but a few.
A look through your oddments box should produce many more ideas.

A SIMPLE POCKET

Materials needed
A small scrap of skirt fabric
A small piece of lace
Sewing cotton to match

Making the pocket
Cut the pocket into the shape and size required allowing for turnings on all the edges.
Press the turnings to the wrong side of the fabric and neaten them (figure 10).

10

Sew the pocket onto the skirt. Make a handkerchief by cutting the lace into a square of correct size for the pocket. Fold the handkerchief and insert it into the pocket (figure 11).

11

One or two rows of ribbon or ric-rac braid sewn or glued around the lower third of the skirt adds eye-catching detail (figure 12).

12

STENCILLING A PLAIN FABRIC SKIRT

Materials needed
Fabric paint
A soft brush
A paper doily
A stencil is a piece of paper or card with a pattern cut out of it.

When this is laid onto the fabric and brushed over with fabric paint the cut-out pattern is reproduced onto the fabric. The doily is a ready-made stencil (figure 13).

13

Experiment first on a waste piece of fabric until you get the pattern you require.
Lay the cut-out skirt on a flat surface covered with newspaper.
Place the stencil over the skirt in the place you wish to print the design.
Load a clean brush with the fabric paint and brush over the stencil (figure 14).

14

Pick the stencil off the fabric and repeat the process until you have a finished design.
Follow the maker's instructions for sealing the fabric paint once your design is complete.

Pull up the gathering thread on the middle tier so that it fits around the lower edge of the top tier.
With right sides together sew the middle tier to the top tier (figure 16).

16

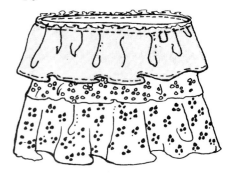

Finish the skirt and the waistband as for the skirt on page 10.

A THREE-TIERED SKIRT

Measuring
Measure the doll as for the simple skirt with a waistband (page 10).
Decide on the finished depth of the skirt.
Divide this measurement by three.
Add 2 cm (¾ in.) for the seam allowances.
The length of the top tier is the same as for the skirt with a waistband.
Make the length of the middle tier twice as long as the length of the top tier.
Make the length of the bottom tier twice as long as the length of the middle tier.

Materials needed
Estimated length of patterned fabric
Sewing cotton to match
A press-stud

MAKING THE SKIRT

With right sides together fold the top tier in half and sew halfway up the short sides.
With right sides together sew the middle and bottom tiers in the same way, sewing all the way up the side seams.
Run a gathering thread around the top long edge on each of the tiers.
Pull up the gathering thread of the bottom tier so that it fits around the lower edge of the middle tier.
With right sides together sew the bottom tier to the middle tier (figure 15).

15

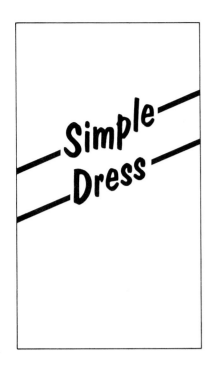

Simple Dress

MEASURING

The front
Write down all the measurements as you work.

Using figure B as a guide measure from the centre under-arm A, across to the centre front B.

Add 1 cm (³⁄₈ in.) for the seam allowance, and .5 cm (¼ in.) to allow for the ease of fit. If the dress is too tight it will be almost impossible to get it on and off the doll.

Measure from the top of the outside shoulder C, in a straight line to F.

The point F is level with point A.

Add 1 cm (³⁄₈ in.) seam allowance.

Measure from point A, to point F, and add 1.5 cm (⁵⁄₈ in.).

Measure from point A, to point G, and add 1.5 cm (⁵⁄₈ in.).

Measure from the top of the neck edge on the shoulder line, point D, down to point G, and add 1 cm (³⁄₈ in.) seam allowance.

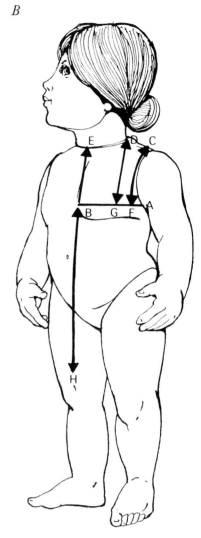

B

Measure from the centre front neck edge E, down to point B.
Measure from where you decide the lower edge of the dress should be (H).
Add 2 cm (¾ in.) for the hem.

The dress back
Measure the doll's back in the same way as for the front but add 3 cm (1¼ in.) to the back measurement A–B instead of 1 cm (³⁄₈ in.).
This is to allow for the overlap and turnings on the centre back fastening.

17

place on fold

front cut 1

back cut 2

not to scale

MAKING THE PAPER PATTERN

Materials needed

Stiff paper
A ruler
A pencil
A pair of scissors
Rule up the sheet of stiff paper into squares. The paper must be large enough to allow the patterns to fit onto it. The size of the squares will depend on the size of the doll. A small doll will require 1 cm (3/8 in.) squares, while a large doll will require 2.5 cm (1 in.) squares or 5 cm (2 in.) squares.
Using figure 17 as a guide, transfer the measurements onto the paper.
Plot points A, B, F, and G, first.
At point J, curve away the hem line to prevent the sides from drooping.
This only applies to flared skirts.
Label each pattern piece carefully.
Cut out the pattern.
If the pattern is made carefully it can be used again and again.

Materials needed

The paper pattern
Estimated length of cotton, corduroy, or thin woollen fabric
Sewing cotton to match
Bias binding
Three press-studs
Rubber-solution glue (optional).

Making the dress

Pin the paper pattern to the fabric making sure that the centre front is placed on the fold of the fabric (If corduroy is being used be sure to have the nap running the same way on all the pieces).

Cut out the dress.
With right sides together sew the dress backs to the front at the shoulder and side seams (figure 18).

18

Neaten the raw edges and press the seams open.
Turn in the 1 cm (3/8 in.) seam allowance on the back edges. of the dress and sew them into place (figure 19).

19

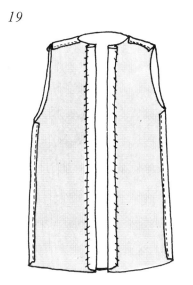

Fit the dress onto the doll.
Trim the armhole and neck edges where necessary.
Cut two lengths of bias binding to fit around the arm-holes allowing 1 cm (3/8 in.) for the turnings.
Join the ends of the armhole bias strips to form two circles.
With right sides together sew the bias binding to the arm-hole and neck edges, turning the ends back at the centre back edges (figure 20).

20

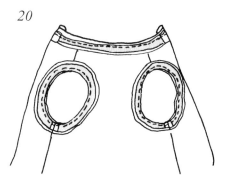

Turn the bias binding to the wrong side of the dress and slip stitch it into place (figure 21).

21

Sew the press-studs to the centre back edges.
Turn up and sew the hem.

DECORATING A PLAIN DRESS

Appliqué

In appliqué one piece of material is placed upon another to form a pattern. As the doll's clothes will be washed it is advisable to use a similar type of fabric to the one used for the dress.
Cut out your design and place it in the desired position on the dress.
Tack it into place.
Using a contrasting thread, stitch the appliqué to the dress using buttonhole stitch (see figure 22).

The appliqué may be glued to the dress but this will not look as effective, or last as long. These are a few ideas for appliqué patterns.

22

MEASURING

The front bodice

Write down all the measurements as you work
Using figure C as a guide,

measure from the top outside shoulder point C, in a straight line to point A.
Add 2 cm (⅜ in.) for the seam allowances.
Measure from point A, across to point B.
Add 1 cm (⅜ in.) for the seam allowance.
Measure from the top shoulder neck edge D, down to point G.
Add 2 cm (¾ in.) to this measurement.
Measure from point A, to point G, and add 1 cm (⅜ in.) for the seam allowance.
Measure from point B, up to where you decide the neck line of the pinafore will be (point E). Add 1 cm (⅜ in.).

The bodice back

Measure the doll's back in the same way as for the front.
Add 2.5 cm (1 in.) to the back measurement A—B instead of 1 cm (⅜ in.).
This is to allow for the back turnings and the overlap on the back fastening.

C

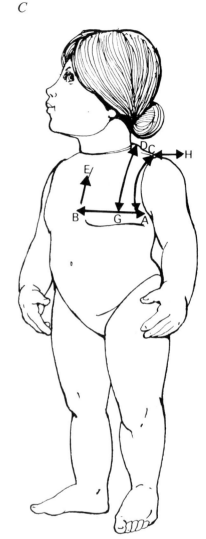

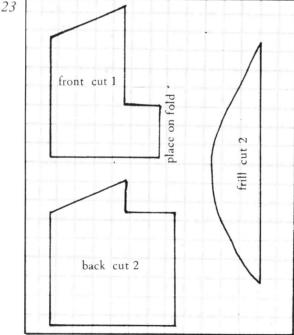

23

The skirt

Measure for the skirt in the same way as for the skirt on page 9.
When measuring the depth of the skirt be sure to measure from the line at the bottom of the bodice and *not* from the waist.

The arm frill

Measure from point A, over the doll's shoulder to the equivalent point on the back.
Add half of this measurement

16

again and 2 cm (¾ in.) seam allowance.
Measure from the outside shoulder C, to where you decide the outer edge of the frill should be (point H).
Add 2 cm (¾ in.) seam allowance.

Making the paper pattern
Using figure 23 as a guide, make the paper pattern in the same way as in the previous chapter.
There are four pattern pieces, the front bodice, the back bodice, the arm frill and the skirt.

Materials needed
The paper pattern
Estimated length of cotton fabric
Sewing cotton to match
Two press-studs
Rubber-solution glue (optional)

Making the pinafore-dress
Follow the instructions for the skirt on page 9 (figure 5 for skirt with waistband).
With right sides together sew the back bodices to the front bodice at the shoulder seams.
Turn under 1 cm (⅜ in.) on each of the back bodice centre edges.
Sew into place (figure 24).

24

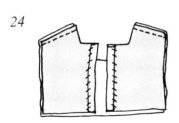

Cut a piece of bias binding 1 cm (⅜ in.) longer than the neck edge of the bodice.
With right sides together sew the bias binding to the neck

edge of the bodice, turning in the ends of the bias at the centre back edges.
Ease at the corners.
Clip the four corners down to the stitching (figure 25).

25

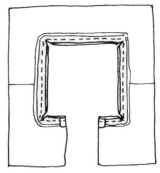

Turn the bias to the wrong side of the bodice and slip stitch it into place.
Turn under 1 cm (⅜ in.) on the curved edge of the frill, making tucks where necessary to ensure the hem lies flat.
Run a gathering thread along the straight edge of the frill (figure 26).

26

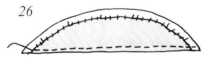

With the straight edges together, place the frill onto the bodice with the right sides together.
Leaving 1 cm (⅜ in.) free at each end of the bodice, pull up the gathering thread so that the frill fits along the armhole edge of the bodice.
Cut a piece of bias binding the same length as the armhole edge of the bodice.
Place this strip over the frill along the armhole stitching line.
Sew this seam (figure 27).

27

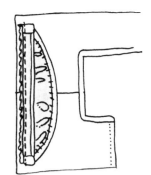

Turn the bias binding to the wrong side of the bodice and slip stitch it into place.
Pull up the gathering thread on the skirt so that the gathered fabric fits the doll around the chest where the measurement for the width of the skirt was taken.
Allow an extra 1 cm (⅜ in.) for the back fastening overlap
With right sides together pin the front bodice to the front of the skirt and the back bodice to the back of the skirt.
Adjust the gathers so that the back and the front of the pinafore-dress are gathered, leaving the underarms straight.
Sew the pinafore skirt to the bodice (figure 28).

28

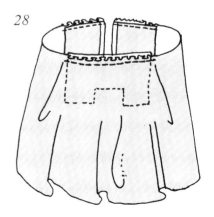

Neaten the edges of the seam, sewing down the plain under-arm sections of the skirt.

Sew the press-studs to the back fastening.
Turn up the hem and glue or sew it into place.
Press the finished pinafore-dress.

Adding a frill

A frill around the base of the pinafore dress adds extra detail and makes the pinafore look more exciting.
It is easy to do and yet gives an expensive and professional finish.

Materials needed

A straight length of fabric (either left over from the pinafore-dress or in a contrasting material). This should measure twice the length of the lower edge of the skirt.
At the very least the depth of the frill should be one-third of the skirt depth.
Add 2 cm (¾ in.) to the depth of the frill for the seam allowances.
A length of ribbon or braid.

Making the frill

Join the strip together at the short sides.
Turn up 1 cm (⅜ in.) on one long edge of the frill.
Run a gathering thread along the other long edge (figure 29).

29

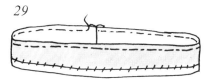

Pull up the gathering thread so that the gathered frill fits around the hem edge of the pinafore skirt.
Place the wrong side of the frill onto the right side of the skirt, matching the lower edges.

Adjust the gathers and sew the frill into place.
Sew a band of ribbon or braid over the rough edges (figure 30).

30

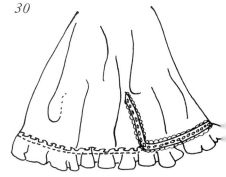

Alternatively you could turn under both the long edges of the frill and simply machine the frill into place so that the upper edge of the frill becomes a decoration.

18

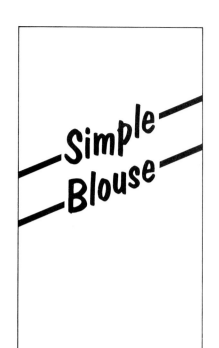

MEASURING

The front and the back

Write down all the measurements as you work. Using figure D as a guide, measure the doll around the chest. Halve this measurement and add 2.5 cm (1 in.) to it. Measure from the outer shoulder point A, down to level with the doll's underarm point B. Add 2 cm (¾ in.) to this.

Measure from the centre of the underarm point C, across the chest to point B, adding 1.5 cm (⅝ in.).

Measure from point A, down to where the finished edge of the blouse will be. Add 2.5 cm (1 in.).

D

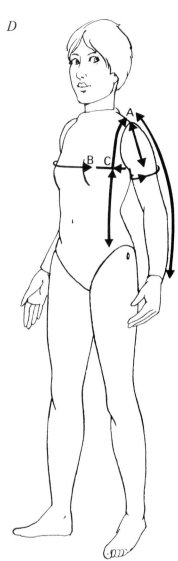

As the size of doll's head varies considerably from doll to doll, check that the neck edge when sewn will pass over the doll's head. If it will not, add the necessary extra amount to the chest measurement.

The sleeve

Measure from the top of the shoulder point A, down the outer edge of the arm to level with the underarm point C, adding 1 cm (⅜ in.). Measure around the arm on a level with

31

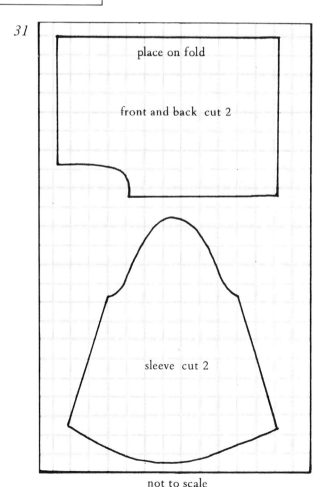

place on fold

front and back cut 2

sleeve cut 2

not to scale

19

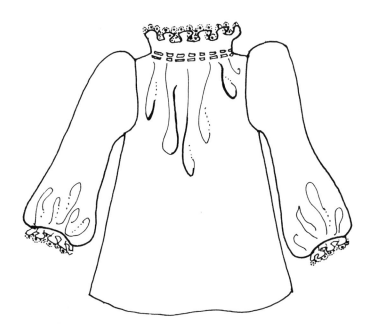

Run a gathering thread around the top edge of the sleeve (figure 33).

33

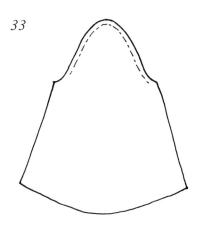

Draw up the gathering thread so that the sleeve fits into the armhole of the blouse (figure 34).

34

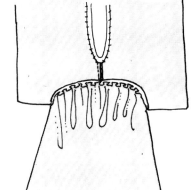

point C. Add 2.5 cm (1 in.) to this measurement.
Measure from point A, down the outer edge of the arm (passing over the bend in the arm) down to the wrist. Add 2 cm (¾ in.) to this measurement.

Making the paper pattern
Using figure 31 as a guide, make the paper pattern in the same way as on page 14. There are two pattern pieces, the blouse front and back, and the sleeve.

Materials needed
The paper pattern
Estimated length of cotton lawn
Sewing cotton to match
Shirring elastic
Lace for the neck and sleeve edges

Making the blouse
Pin the pattern to the fabric.
Cut out the blouse.
With right sides together sew the blouse back and front pieces together at the top of the sleeve opening.
Turn under a small hem around the neck edge of the blouse.
Stitch into place (figure 32).

32

Stitch this seam twice.
With right sides together sew up the side and underarm seams.
Clip the curve on this seam down to the stitching (figure 35).

35

Turn up the hem on the lower
edge of the blouse and sleeves.
Stitch into place.
Run two rows of double
shirring elastic around the
neck and sleeve edges far
enough in from the edge to
make the cuffs and collar
(figure 36).

36

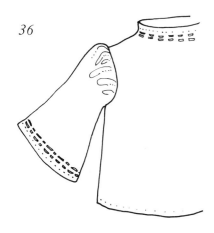

Sew the lace around the neck
and sleeve edges.
Draw up the shirring elastic so
that it fits around the doll's
neck and wrists.
Make sure that the neck edge
will stretch open enough to
allow for the blouse to pass
over the doll's head.
Fasten the elastic off securely.
By lengthening the blouse it
becomes a smock-dress.

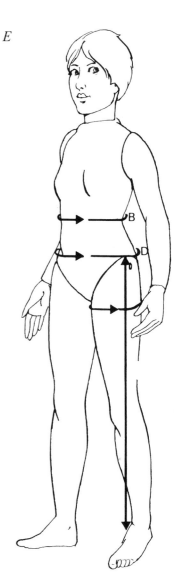

E

waist. Halve this measurement and add 2.5 cm (1 in.) for the seam allowances. Measure the doll around the hips.

Halve this measurement and add 3 cm (1¼ in.) for the seam allowances and ease of movement when the doll is bent into a sitting position. Measure around the top of the doll's leg and add 2.5 cm (1 in.).

Measure from the side of the doll's waist point B, in a straight line down to the level of where the hip measurement was taken, (point D). Add 1.5 cm (⅝ in.).

Measure from point B, down to where the finished bottom of the trousers will be. Add 2.5 cm (1 in.) to this.

Make sure that the doll's foot will fit through the chosen finished width of the trouser leg.

MEASURING

Using figure E as a guide, measure around the doll's

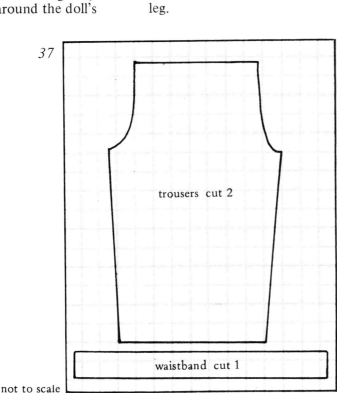

37

trousers cut 2

waistband cut 1

not to scale

The waistband
The length
Measure the doll's waist and add 2 cm (¾ in.) for the seam allowances and the front fastening overlap.
The depth
Decide on the finished depth of the waistband and double this measurement.
Add 2 cm (¾ in.) to this for the seam allowances.

Making the paper pattern
Using figure 37 as a guide, make the paper pattern as on page 14. There are two main pattern pieces, the trousers and the waistband.

Materials needed
The paper pattern
Estimated length of corduroy, felt or strong cotton fabric
Sewing cotton to match
Two press-studs

Making the trousers
Pin the paper pattern to the fabric.
Cut out the trousers.
With right sides together join the two trouser pieces together at the curved seams, leaving half of the front seam open for the front fastening (figure 38).

38

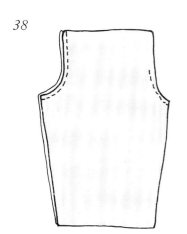

With right sides together sew up the inside leg seam.
Clip this seam to the stitching around the curve (figure 39).
With right sides together fold the waistband in half length-wise.
Press up the seam allowance in one long side of the waist-band.
Stitch the two short ends of the waistband (figure 40).

39

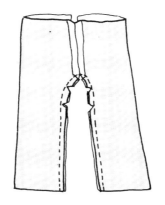

40

Turn the band inside out.
With right sides together place the unturned edge of the waistband onto the outside waist edge of the trousers.
Sew this seam (figure 41).

41

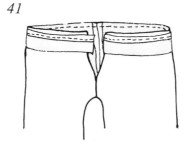

Turn up the waistband and slip stitch the turned edge to the inside of the trousers.
Sew the press-studs to the front of the waistband and the front opening.
Turn up the hem on the bottom of the trouser legs and hem into place.

TURNING A PAIR OF TROUSERS INTO A PAIR OF DUNGAREES

Measuring
The bib
Measure the chest of the doll and decide on the size of the rectangle or square for the bib. Add 1 cm (⅜ in.) to all the sides.
The straps
Measure from where the finished top of the bib will be, over the doll's shoulder and diagonally across the back down to the back waistline. Add 4 cm (1½ in.) to this measurement for the turnings and attachment.
Decide on the finished width of the straps. Double this measurement and add 2 cm (¾ in.) for the turnings.
Using these measurements make the paper pattern.

Making the Dungarees
Make the trousers in the same way as on page 22 *but* make the opening at the back instead of at the front.
Cut out two bib pieces and two straps using the same fabric as that of the trousers.
With right sides together leaving one side open sew the two bib pieces together.
Turn the bib inside out, through the open side.
Press the bib and slip stitch the opening closed (figure 42).

42

Fold in the seam allowance on the long edges of the straps.

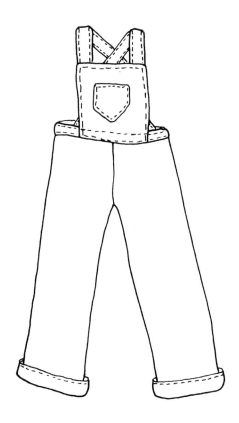

PANTALOONS

These can be made by adapting the trouser pattern.
Make the legs of the trousers wider and the length to just below the doll's knee.
The bottoms of the trousers are gathered into a band in the same way as a skirt is gathered into a waistband (see page 10).
Sew a press-stud to the legbands to fasten them around the doll's leg.

Fold the straps in half, wrong sides together, and sew down (figure 43).

43

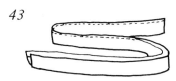

Sew the bib to the centre front edge of the trousers waistband.
Turn in the ends of the straps and slip stitch into place.
Sew the straps to the top outside corners of the bib.
Sew the press-studs to the ends of the straps and to the back waistband.

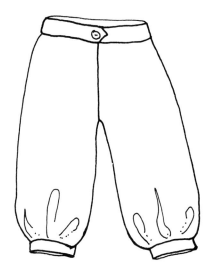

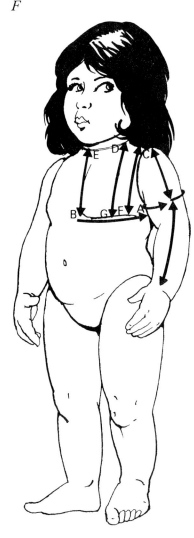

F

MEASURING

The front
Write down all the measurements as you work.
Using figure F as a guide, measure from the centre underarm point A, across to the centre front point B.
Add 4 cm (1½ in.) to this measurement.
Measure from the top of the outside shoulder point C, down in a straight line to point F. (This point is level with the doll's underarm).
Add 1 cm (⅜ in.) to this measurement.
Measure from point A, to point F, and add 1 cm (⅜ in.).
Measure from point A, to point G, and add 1 cm (⅜ in.).
Measure from the top of the neck edge on the shoulder-line, point D, down to point G.
Add 1 cm (⅜ in.).
Measure from the centre front neck edge point E, down to point B. Add 1 cm (⅜ in.) to this measurement.

Measure from point E, down to where the finished edge of the shirt will be. Add 2 cm (¾ in.) to this measurement.

The back
Measure the doll's back in the same way as for the front, but here you add 1 cm (⅜ in.) to the measurement A, to B, instead of 4 cm (1½ in.).

The sleeve
Measure from the top of the shoulder point C, down the outside of the arm to level

with the doll's underarm, point A.
Add 1 cm (⅜ in.) to this measurement.
Measure around the doll's arm on a level with point A. Add 1.5 cm (⅝ in.) to this measurement.
Measure from point C, down the outside of the arm, passing over the bend in the doll's arm, down to the wrist.
Add 2 cm (¾ in.) to this measurement.

The cuff
Measure around the doll's wrist and add 1.5 cm (⅝ in.) to this measurement.
Decide on the finished depth of the cuff. Double this measurement and add 2 cm (¾ in.) for the seam allowances.

The collar
Measure around the doll's neck and add 2 cm (¾ in.).
Decide on the finished depth of the collar and add 2 cm (¾ in.) to this.
It is always advisable to make a preliminary collar from newspaper.
This ensures a good fit.

Making the paper pattern
Using figure 44 as a guide, make the paper pattern in the same way as on page 14.
There are five pattern pieces, the shirt front, back, sleeve, collar and cuff.

Materials needed
The paper pattern
Estimated length of cotton fabric
Sewing cotton to match
Five press-studs
Three small buttons

Making the shirt
Pin the paper pattern to the fabric.

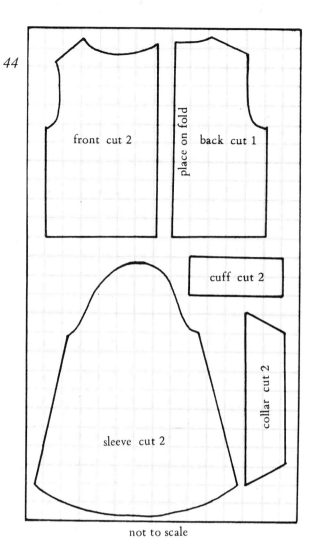

44

front cut 2

place on fold

back cut 1

cuff cut 2

collar cut 2

sleeve cut 2

not to scale

Cut out the shirt.
With right sides together sew the shirt fronts to the back at the shoulder and side seams.
Neaten the front edges (figure 45).

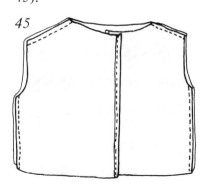

45

With right sides together stitch around the outer edge of the collar pieces leaving the neck edge open.
Trim the seam and clip the corners diagonally (figure 46).

46

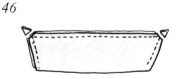

Turn the collar inside out, pushing the corners out with an orange stick.
Press the collar.
Turn in 2 cm (¾ in.) on the

front edges of the shirt. Tack these in place at the neck edge. With right sides together stitch the underside of the neck edge of the collar to the neck edge of the shirt leaving 0.5 cm (¼ in.) free at both the centre front neck edges (figure 47).

47

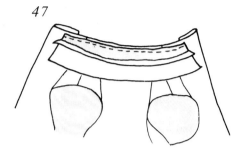

Turn under the seam allowance on the upper edge of the collar and slip stitch it to the wrong side of the neck edge of the shirt (figure 48).

48

Neaten the shirt front neck edges.
With right sides together sew the sleeve seam, leaving 2 cm (¾ in.) open at the wrist.
Run a gathering thread around the top and lower edges of the sleeve (figure 49).
With right sides together pin the centre top of the sleeve to the outer shoulder seam of the shirt.

49

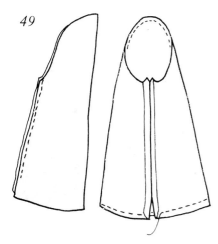

Draw up the gathering thread so that the sleeve fits into the shirt armhole.
Ease the gathers so that the sleeve fits as flatly as possible. Stitch this seam twice (figure 50).

50

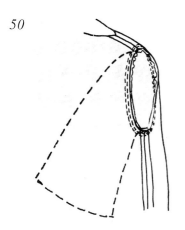

Turn in the seam allowance on the long edges of the cuffs. With right sides together fold the cuff in half lengthwise. Sew the two short ends. Turn the cuff inside out. (figure 51).

51

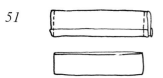

Draw up the gathering thread so that the sleeve is 1 cm ($\frac{3}{8}$ in.) shorter than the length of the cuff.
Fit the sleeve into the cuff. Stitch the cuff to the sleeve (figure 52).

52

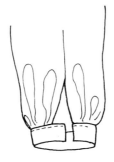

Turn up the lower edge of the shirt and hem into place.
Sew the press-studs to the front opening and to the cuffs.
Sew the buttons to the front of the shirt.
A white collar and cuffs on a plain or patterned shirt adds a clean crisp appearance.
A pocket can be sewn to the front of the shirt.

MEASURING

The front

Using figure G as a guide, measure from the shoulder neck edge, point A, down to where the finished bottom of the cape will be. Add 3 cm (1¼ in.) to this measurement for the hem and seam allowances.
Measure from the centre of the outside arm, point B, on a level with the underarm across to the front, point D. Add 2 cm (¾ in.) to this.
Measure down from point A, to point D, which is level with the underarm.
Add 1 cm (⅜ in.) to this measurement.
Measure from point B, in a straight line, across to the centre front point E. Add 2 cm (¾ in.) to this.

The back

Measure the back in exactly the same way as for the front, adding the same allowances

except for the measurement B to D. Add 1 cm (⅜ in.) to this instead of 2 cm (¾ in.).

The hood

Measure from the centre front base of the neck, point F, up around the side of the doll's head to the top centre front of the head, point G.
Add 2 cm (¾ in.) to this measurement.
Measure from point G, back along the centre top of the doll's head to point H, at the back of the head.
Add 2 cm (¾ in.) to this measurement.
Measure from point F, around

the base of the neck to the centre back point J.
Add 2 cm (¾ in.) to this measurement.

Making the paper pattern

Using figure 53 as a guide, make the paper pattern as on page 14.
There are three pattern pieces, the back, the front and the hood.

Materials needed

The paper pattern
Estimated length of corduroy, soft wool or velvet
Estimated length of lining fabric

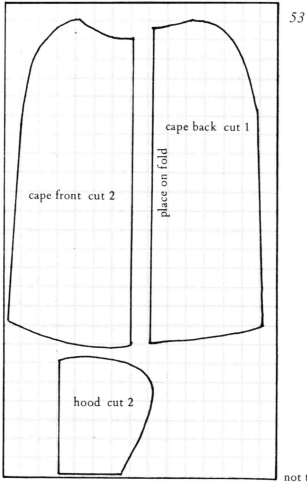

53

cape back cut 1

place on fold

cape front cut 2

hood cut 2

not to scale

G

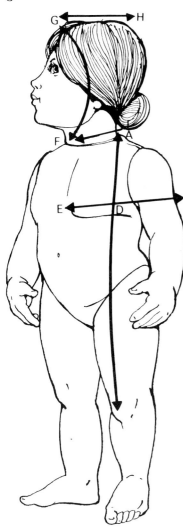

Sewing cotton to match
Two lengths of cord

Making the cape

Pin the pattern to the fabric.
Cut out the cape pieces twice,
one in the main fabric and
one in the contrasting fabric.
(If you are using corduroy or
velvet remember to have the
pile running the same way on
all the pattern pieces.)
With right sides together sew
the cape back to the fronts at
the side seams.

Clip the curves down to the
stitching.
Trim the cape neck edge and
clip (figure 54).

54

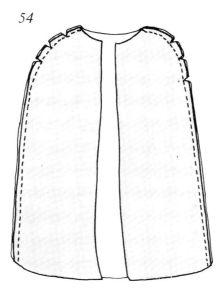

With right sides together sew
the hood together at the back
seam.
Clip the curve (figure 55).

55

With right sides together sew
the hood to the cape at the
neck edge.
Clip the curve (figure 56).
Press under the hem allowance
on the bottom edge of the
cape.
Make the lining in exactly the
same way.
With right sides together place
the two capes together

56

matching the edges and seams.
Sew the capes together around
the outer edge, leaving the
bottom edge open.
Clip the curve (figure 57).

57

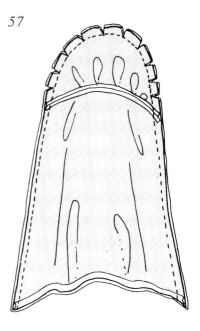

Turn the cape inside out and
slip stitch the two hems
together.
Sew a piece of cord to each of
the front neck edges.

Trimming the Cape

A cape can be worn for everyday wear or for evenings. If the cape is made out of velvet, a length of fur placed around the edge of the hood gives it a very expensive look.

Cut a length of fur to the same length as the face edge of the hood and twice the width of the required finished depth.

Fur should be cut with a craft knife.

Cut the fur from the inside, just slicing through the skin, *not* cutting the fur.

Fold the fur strip in half lengthwise and glue or sew it around the face edge of the hood.

A similar fur strip can be sewn or glued around the base of the cape.

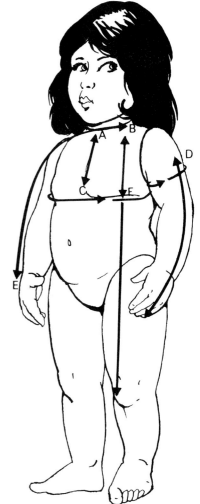

H

NIGHTDRESS

Measuring

The yoke
Using figure H as a guide, measure the width of the doll's neck. Halve this measurement and take off 1 cm (⅜ in.)
This is the radius of the opening for the neck.
Measure from the centre front base of the neck, point A, down in a straight line to where the finished edge of the yoke will be, point C.
Add this to the radius of the neck-opening and add a further 2 cm (¾ in.) for the seam allowances.

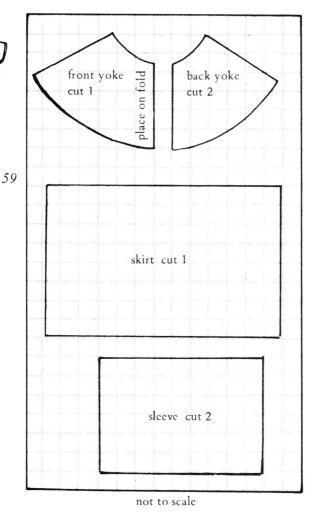

58

59

front yoke
cut 1

place on fold

back yoke
cut 2

skirt cut 1

sleeve cut 2

not to scale

The back and front
Measure the doll around the chest and add 2 cm (¾ in.) for the seams.

The sleeve
Measure around the top of the doll's arm. Add half as much again plus 2 cm (¾ in.).
Measure from where the finished lower edge of the yoke will be at the top of the arm, point D, down the arm to the fingertips. Add 2 cm (¾ in.).

31

Making the paper pattern

Make a preliminary pattern out of newspaper for the yoke. Use figure 59 as a guide.
Using a pair of compasses draw the neckhole circle onto the newspaper.
Draw the outer circle.
Cut out the circle.
Cut from the outer edge to the centre of the circle and cut out the neck opening.
Fit the yoke onto the doll.
Cut away a V-shaped piece from the shoulders to give the slope of the shoulders.
Place the preliminary pattern pieces onto a piece of stiff paper and draw around them with a pencil allowing 1 cm (⅜ in.) at the shoulder edges and 2 cm (¾ in.) at the centre front opening.
Using figure 59 as a guide make the paper pattern as on page 14.
There are four pattern pieces, the back yoke, the front yoke, the front and back, and the sleeve.

Materials needed

Estimated length of fine cotton lawn
Sewing cotton to match
Shirring elastic
Three buttons
Lace for the trimmings
Buttonhole thread

Making the nightdress

Pin the pattern to the fabric.
Cut out the nightdress.
With right sides together join the yoke fronts to the back at the shoulder seams (figure 60).

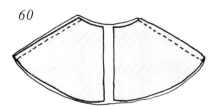

60

Join the other yoke in the same way.
Press in the seam allowance on the outer edge on one of the yokes.
With right sides together sew the two yokes together at the neck and centre front edges. Clip the curve to the stitching and trim the corners (figure 61).

61
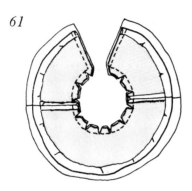

Turn the yoke inside out and press.
Sew the sleeves to the front and back of the nightdress (figure 62).

62
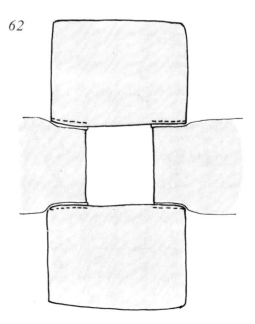

Join the side and sleeve seams. Turn up the lower edge of the sleeve and sew into place.
Run a gathering thread around the top edge of the nightdress (figure 63).

63

With right sides together match the centre front, the centre back and the shoulders of the nightdress to the corresponding points on the

unpressed outer edge of the yoke.
Draw up the gathers so that the nightdress fits around the yoke (figure 64).

64

Sew the nightdress to the yoke. Press the yoke up and slip stitch the pressed edge of the inner yoke over the seam line on the inside of the nightdress (figure 65).

65

Turn up the hem and sew into place.
Make loops of buttonhole thread down one side of the front opening (figure 66).
Run a row of double shirring elastic around the wrists of the nightdress.
Pull up the elastic so that it fits the doll's wrist.

Sew the buttons to the front opening, matching them to the loops.
Trim the neck, sleeve and yoke edges with the lace.

66

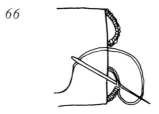

A REVERSIBLE MOB CAP

Measuring
Measure around the doll's head.
Halve this measurement. This is the radius of the circle (figure 67).

67

Making the paper pattern
Using a pair of compasses set at the correct radius, draw a circle.

Materials needed
Two circles of cotton fabric (one plain, one patterned)
Sewing cotton to match
Shirring elastic
Lace or broderie Anglaise (to the measurement of the outer edge of the circle.

Making the cap
Press under 1 cm ($\frac{3}{8}$ in.) from the right side to the wrong on

33

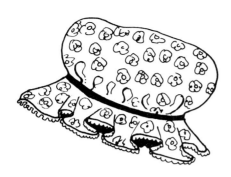

the outer edge of each of the circles (figure 68).

68

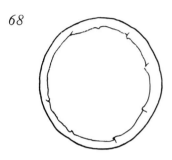

With wrong sides together, place the two circles together. Insert the lace between the outer edges (figure 69).

69

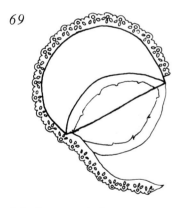

Stitch around the outer edge. Using double shirring elastic sew two rows of running stitches around the crown of the cap 2.5 cm (1 in.) from the outside edge (figure 70).

70

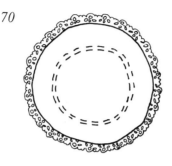

Draw up the gathering thread so that it fits around the doll's head.
Fasten off the elastic securely. A band of ribbon can be put around the crown to hide the gathering stitches.

VEST, PANTS AND A BRA

Measuring the pants
Measure the doll's waist. Halve this measurement and add 2 cm (¾ in.) for the seam allowances.
Measure from the doll's waist down to the top of the leg.

Add 2 cm (¾ in.) to this measurement.
Measure the width and the length of the space between the doll's legs.
Add 2 cm (¾ in.) to the width measurement.

Measuring the vest
Measure the doll around the chest.
Halve this measurement and add 2 cm (¾ in.).
Measure from the doll's shoulder down to where the finished lower edge of the vest will be.
Add 2 cm (¾ in.) for the hem.

Measuring the bra
Add 5 cm (2 in.) to the chest measurement.
Decide on the finished depth of the bra and add 2 cm (¾ in.) for the seams.

Making the paper pattern
Using (figure 71) as a guide, make the paper pattern as on page 14.

Materials needed
Estimated length of stretch cotton fabric (an old sock or vest can be used instead)
Sewing cotton to match
Shirring elastic
A large-eyed needle
A length of ribbon
A press-stud
Lace edging

Making the vest
Pin the paper pattern to the fabric.
Cut out the garments.

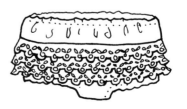

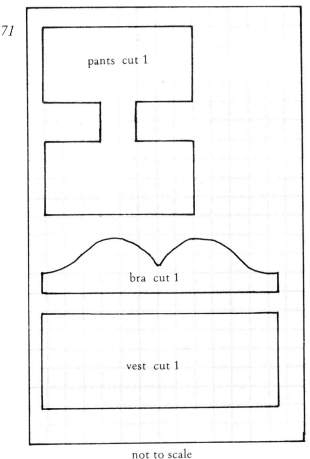

71

pants cut 1

bra cut 1

vest cut 1

not to scale

74

Fit the vest onto the doll.
Trim the neck and armhole
edges to the required shape.
Turn in the armhole, neck and
lower edges of the vest.
Sew these in place (figure 75).

75

The armhole and neck edges
can be trimmed with lace.

Join the pants together at the
side seams (figure 72).

72

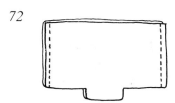

Fit the pants onto the doll.
Trim the legholes to the
required shape.
If bikini pants are required
trim the top of the pants down.
Turn in the top and leghole
edges.
Stitch these in place, leaving
an opening for the threading
of the elastic (figure 73).

73

Thread the top and leg hems
with double shirring elastic.
Pull up the elastic to fit the
waist and legs of the doll.
Fasten off securely.
If the pants are for a baby doll
three rows of lace sewn to the
back of the pants makes them
prettier.

Making the vest
Pin the vest to the fabric.
Cut out the vest.
Join the vest together at the
side seams, leaving an opening
for the armhole (figure 74).

Making the bra

Pin the pattern to the fabric.
Cut out the bra.
Sew two darts at the front of the bra.
These form the cups (figure 76).

76

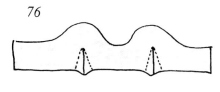

Turn in the seam allowances on all the edges of the bra.
Sew into place.
Cut two lengths of ribbon for the straps.
Sew these to the top of the cups and to the back of the bra.
Sew a press-stud to the back fastening.

A PETTICOAT

Measuring

The top
This is exactly the same as the bra.

The skirt
Measure from where the bottom edge of the bra comes to on the doll down to where the finished lower edge of the petticoat will be.
Add 2 cm (¾ in.) to this measurement.
Measure the doll around the hips.
Add 4 cm (1½ in.) to this measurement for the seam allowances and the fullness of the skirt.

Making the paper pattern

Using figure 77 as a guide, make the paper pattern as on page 14.
There are two pattern pieces, the bra and the skirt.

Materials needed

Estimated length of lawn, nylon or taffeta fabric
Sewing cotton to match
Two lengths of ribbon

Making the petticoat

Pin the pattern to the fabric.
Cut out the petticoat.
Make the top as for the bra, leaving the lower edge unturned.
With right sides together, join the skirt at the side seams.
Make a cut in the top edge of the centre back of the skirt.
Neaten this cut (figure 78).

78

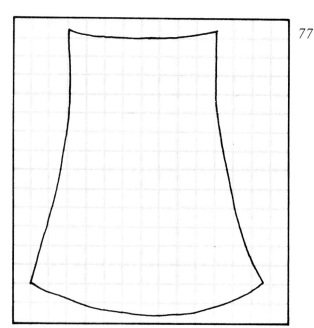

77

With right sides together join
the bra to the skirt (figure 79).

79

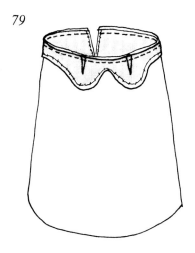

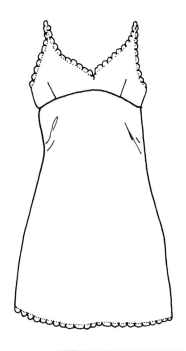

Sew a press-stud to the back
fastening.
Turn up a 0.5 cm (¼ in.) hem
on the lower edge of the
petticoat.
Tack this in place.
Using double thread of
matching or contrasting colour,
take five or six small running
stitches along the hem. Make a
stitch over the edge of the
hem. Pull this tight.
Make a similar over-stitch to
fasten the first.
Make another row of running
stitches and another over-
stitch. Continue in this way
around the hem (figure 80).

80

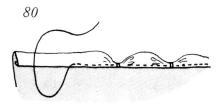

This edging is called shell-
edging and can be used on any
fine fabric. It is especially
good for lingerie.

81

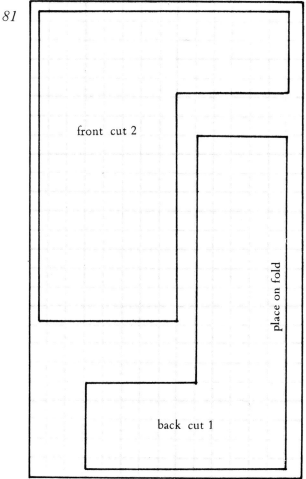

front cut 2

place on fold

back cut 1

not to scale

37

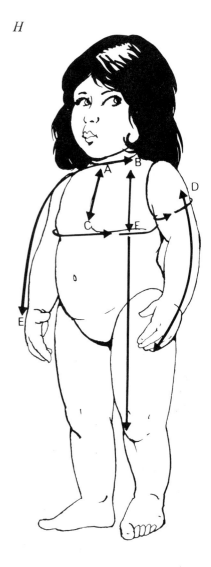

H

A WRAP-OVER DRESSING-GOWN

Measuring

The front
Using figure H as a guide,
measure from the side of the
neck point B, across the body
and down the arm to the wrist,
point E.
Measure from the top of the
shoulder down to where the
lower edge of the gown will
be.

Measure from the shoulder in a straight line down to below the armpit, point F.
Add 2 cm (¾ in.) to this measurement.

The back
Measure from one wrist up the arm and across the shoulder to the centre of the neck.
The other measurements are the same as those for the front.

Making the paper pattern
Using figure 81 as a guide, make the pattern as on page 14. There are two pattern pieces, the front and the back.

Materials needed
Estimated length of towelling
Sewing cotton to match
Bias binding to match
A length of string

Making the dressing-gown
With right sides together, sew the back to the fronts at the underarm and shoulder seams (figure 82).

82

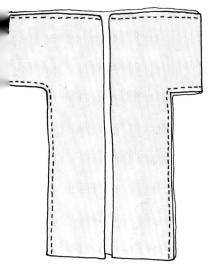

Fit the gown onto the doll.
Trim the front neck edges to the required shape.

Bind the front, sleeve and lower edges with bias binding (figure 83).

83

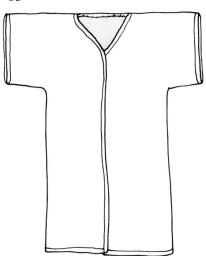

Cut a long strip of fabric for the belt. Make this twice the desired finished width plus 2 cm (¾ in.).
Cut a piece of string 2 cm (¾ in.) longer than the belt.
With right sides together, fold the belt in half lengthwise with the string in the middle. The ends of the string should protrude at either end of the belt.
Sew down one short end of the belt making sure that the string is sewn into the seam.
Sew along the long edge of the belt (figure 84).

84

Pull the string from the open end easing the end of the belt inwards.
This turns the belt inside out (figure 85).

85

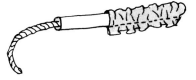

Cut off the string and neaten the ends of the belt.

Modern Uniform and Activity Clothes

Most of the uniforms in this chapter are adapted from patterns in other chapters. It is important to use fabrics which have similar colours to the original uniforms.
The trimmings are also important as they define the rank and service to which the uniforms belong.

THE BASIC UNIFORM

Measuring
Adapt the shirt pattern on page 25 by making the length to below the doll's bottom. The sleeves have no cuffs and are not as full as those of the shirt.
The trousers are the same as those on page 22.
The hats are measured as on page 60.

Materials needed
Estimated length of suitable fabric
Sewing cotton to match
Five press-studs
Five small buttons

Making the uniform

Make the jacket in the same way as the shirt on page 26 making it fit to the doll's waist by using lengthwise darts in the fronts and back (figure 86).

86

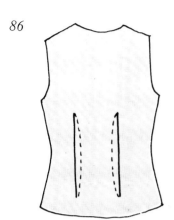

The trousers are made in the same way as those on page 22. Cut out four pockets in the same fabric as the uniform, allowing extra fabric for the turnings and the pleat in the centre of the pocket (figure 87).

87

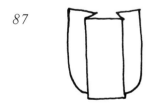

Neaten the edges of the pocket.
Sew one onto either side of the front of the jacket above the waistline and one either side below the waistline.
Cut out a flap and neaten the edges.
Sew this flap over the top of the pocket (figure 88).

88

Sew a press-stud to the underside of the flap and to the front of the pocket.
Cut out four epaulettes allowing for the turnings.
With right sides together sew around the edges leaving the end open (figure 89).

89

Turn inside out and press.
Turn in the end and slipstitch it to the top of the sleeve seam.
Catch the pointed end to the shoulder seam.

Hat for a policeman, traffic warden or army officer

Materials needed
A piece of cardboard
Rubber-solution glue
Felt of the correct colour.

Making the hat
Using figure 90 as a guide, cut out a circle for the top of the hat, a brim and a strip for the band from cardboard.
Place the cardboard pieces onto the felt.
Draw around them allowing 1 cm (³⁄₈ in.) on one long edge of the band and on the inner edge of the brim.

You will need one band and two brims and tops.

90

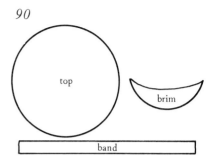

Cut out the pieces and glue a piece to both sides of the brim and the top and to one side of the band (figure 91).

91

Cut V-shaped notches in the felt down to the cardboard on one long edge of the band and the inner edge of the brim (figure 92).

92

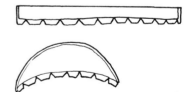

Glue the short ends of the band together.
Glue the notched edge of the band to the top 1 cm (³⁄₈ in.) in from the outer edge (this measurement depends on the size of the doll).
Glue the notched edge of the brim to the front lower edge of the band.

41

Stick black-and white-checked sticky tape around the brim for a policeman's hat, yellow for a traffic warden.
A red band of ribbon is used for the army officer's hat.

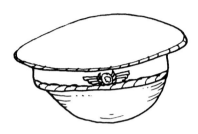

A beret for a soldier

Materials needed
A piece of black felt
Sewing cotton to match
A length of elastic

Making the beret
Cut out the beret.
Make a hem around the outer edge leaving an opening for the threading of the elastic.
Thread the elastic through the hem.
Pull up the elastic to fit the doll's head (figure 93).

OTHER ACCESSORIES

A knapsack
Make this in the same way as the handbag on page 63.
It should be made from thick canvas fabric.
The flap should be made longer and fastened with two straps.
The shoulder straps at the back should be long enough to pass around the shoulders (figure 94).

94

Other equipment such as waterbottles, binoculars and radios can be made from polystyrene and painted the correct colour.
The insignias for the various uniforms can be made from braid or can be embroidered onto the fabric.
Badges can be made from cardboard and covered in silver or gold paper.

AN ASTRONAUT AND DIVER

Measuring
The astronaut's and diver's costumes are similar in shape and construction.
They are basically an all-in-one suit.
Using the shirt pattern from page 26 cut off to 1 cm ($\frac{3}{8}$ in.) below the waistline.
The collar is not needed and the sleeves have no cuff and are not as full as the ones for the shirt.
Use the trouser pattern on page 22 omitting the waist-band.

Materials needed
Estimated length of fibre-glass curtain lining for the astronaut
Estimated length of fawn canvas for the diver
Five press-studs
A length of tape for the waist
A piece of elastic for the waist
Sewing cotton to match.

Making the suit
Make the top of the suit as for the shirt on page 26 omitting the collar and leaving the lower edge unturned.
Make the trousers as on page 22 leaving the top edge unturned.
With right sides together join the top to the trousers at the waistline (figure 95).

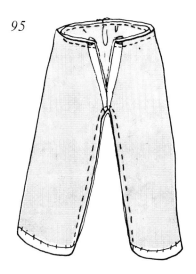

95

Turn under and neaten the
neck and front edges.
Sew a piece of tape around the
inside of the waistline, leaving
the ends free (figure 96).

96

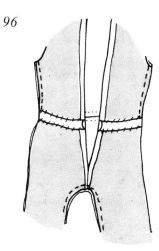

Thread a piece of elastic
between the suit and the tape.
Pull up the elastic so that it
fits the doll's waist.
Fasten off securely at both
ends.
Sew the press-studs to the
front opening.
Using page 62 as a guide, make
a pair of boots and mittens for
the astronaut from the same
fabric as the suit.

The diver's boots and mittens can be made from matching coloured felt.

A piece of foam rubber cut to the same shape as the sole of the boots can be glued to the base of the boot.

This gives the appearance of weight to the boot (figure 97).

97

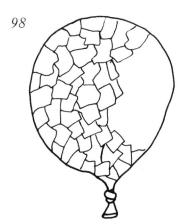

The helmets

Materials needed

A balloon
Newspaper
Wallpaper paste
A paste brush
A piece of Perspex
Two butterfly paperclips
Paint or tin foil

Making the helmets

Blow up the balloon so that it is twice the size of the doll's head.

98

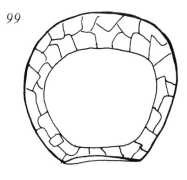

Tie a knot in the end of the balloon.

Paste small pieces of newspaper to the balloon so that it is covered completely.

Keep applying layers of paper until a thickness of approximately 2 mm ($\frac{1}{16}$ in.) is reached (figure 98).

Leave the paper-covered balloon to dry completely.

Cut a hole in the front of the paper on the balloon for visor (this should be oval for the astronaut and round for the diver) (figure 99).

99

Trim the base of the helmet so that it will pass over the doll's head.

Paint the helmet the same colour as the suit.

The astronaut's helmet can be covered with foil.

Cut out a piece of Perspex slightly larger than the hole for the visor.

100

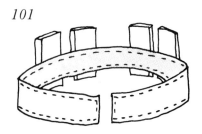

Push the clips through the ends of the Perspex and the sides of the helmet.

Spread the ends of the clips on the inside of the helmet (figure 100).

Make a belt from thick canvas for the diver and glue oblong pieces of Polystyrene to it for the weights (figure 101).

101

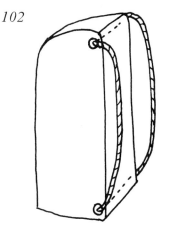

Make the astronaut's pack from Polystyrene cut to the correct size.

Paint this silver.

Make holes through the pack from one side to the other at the top and the bottom.

Thread elastic through the holes to form the shoulder straps (figure 102).

102

44

A RIDING OUTFIT

Measuring
The jacket is made from the
shirt pattern on page 26. The
back must be altered so that it
has a centre back seam.
Remember when doing this to
allow for the seam allowance.
The jodhpurs are made by
adapting the trousers pattern
on page 22.
The lower part of the trousers
must fit tightly around the
doll's leg.
Make sure that the doll's foot
will pass through when the
trousers are sewn, if this is not
possible the lower part of the
inside leg seam can be left
open and fastened with a
press-stud.
Adapt the upper part of the
trousers so that they are full
over the thighs.

Materials needed
Brown or black felt for the
jacket
Fawn woollen fabric for the
jodhpurs
Black felt for the boots and
hat
Sewing cotton to match
Six press-studs
Thread and string

Making the outfit
Make the jacket in the same
way as the jacket on page 41.
Sew the side seams in at the
waistline to give a fitted
appearance (figure 103).
Leave the lower part of the
centre back seam open.
Press this seam to one side.
Sew across the back centre
seam opening (figure 104).
The jodhpurs are made in the
same way as the trousers on
page 22.
Make the boots as on page 62
making them to just below the
knee.

103

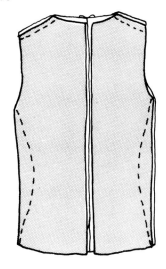

Use iron-on interfacing to strengthen the hat.
A crop can be made from a straight piece of wood.
Cut a piece of leather for the end of the stick and bind it to the stick with thread.
Bind the whole stick with string (figure 106).

106

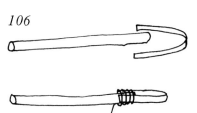

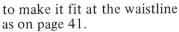

to make it fit at the waistline as on page 41.
Make the sleeves and sew them into the armholes of the tunic in the same way as on page 27. Leave the neck edge unturned.
Fit the tunic onto the doll and cut the front neck edge into a V-shape.
Cut a collar to fit around the neck edge of the tunic that forms a square at the back (figure 107).

107

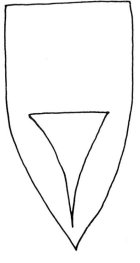

104

The hat is made in the same way as the hat on page 60 but the crown needs to be made higher (figure 105).

A SAILOR

Measuring
The top of this uniform is adapted from the simple dress pattern on page 13.
The sleeve is the same as for the sleeve for the shirt on page 26 making the sleeve less full and omitting the cuff.
The trousers are the same as for the trousers on page 22 but adapted to bell-bottoms by increasing the width of the trouser leg at the lower edge.

Materials needed
Estimated length of navy blue felt
Sewing cotton to match
White embroidery silk
Three press-studs.

Making the suit
Make the top as for the dress on page 13.
Make vertical darts at the front and the back of the suit

With wrong sides together sew the collar to the neck edge (figure 108).

108

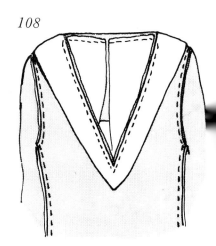

105

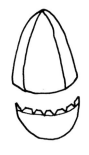

Embroider two rows of chain stitch around the outer edge of the collar (figure 109).

109

Sew the press-studs to the centre back fastening.
Cut a small triangle of felt to fit in the front of the collar at the base of the V.
Sew this in place (figure 110).

110

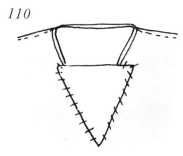

Make the trousers in the same way as for the trousers on page 22.
Make the hat out of felt in the same way as on page 41 omitting the brim.
Embroider or paint the name of the ship the doll belongs to around the band of the hat.
This could be the name of the doll.
For example H.M.S. Peter.

A BALLET COSTUME

Measuring
The bodice is made by
adapting the pattern for the
simple dress on page 13. See
also adaption for the Spanish
costume on page 57.
The length of the bodice is to
the waist with the front
bodice coming to a point at
the centre front to just below
the waistline.
The frills are three times the
doll's waist measurement in
length and to double the
required depth.

Materials needed
Estimated length of white or
pink satin
Estimated length of fine net
(tulle)
White or pink satin ribbon

Sewing cotton to match
Three press-studs

Making the dress
Make the bodice as for the
bodice of the Spanish dress on
page 57.
Trim the neck edge to a curve
which is lower at the front
than at the back (figure 111).

111

48

Bind all the raw edges with the satin ribbon (figure 112).

112

Cut the net into six pieces of the correct size.
Join the short ends of the frills together to form six circles (figure 113).

Make a headband from elastic and attach artificial flowers to it. (These can be made as on page 59 or purchased from a shop.)

113

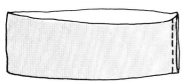

Place the circles one over the other and run a gathering thread around the centre through all the thicknesses (figure 114).

114

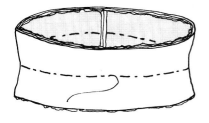

The shoes are made from pink satin with pink ribbons attached for the ties.

Draw up the gathering thread so that the frill fits around the lower edge of the bodice.
Sew the gathered frill to the shaped bodice using tiny stitches.

National Costumes

SCOTTISH

Measuring

Adapt the shirt pattern on page 26 to make the jacket. The jacket length is to just below the waistline.

The sleeves are straight and have no cuff.

The collar is straight and stands up around the neck.

The kilt

Measure the doll around the waist and treble this measurement.

Decide on the finished length of the kilt and add 2 cm (¾ in.) for the turnings.

Materials needed

Estimated length of tartan fabric
Estimated length of black felt for the jacket
Bias binding
Wide white tape
Six black buttons
Six press-studs
White lace for the cuffs and jabot

A length of cord
A piece of white fur
Sewing cotton to match.

Making the jacket
Make the jacket in the same way as for the shirt on page 26. The collar is pressed up so that it stands high around the doll's neck.
Turn up the lower edge of the sleeve and sew a row of gathered lace to the inside of the cuff (figure 115).

Making the kilt
Turn up the hem on one short side of the kilt using a single turn only, leaving the two ends unpleated to allow for the front cross-over panel. Mark out the pleats with pins (figure 116).

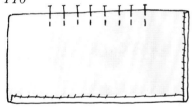

Pleat up the fabric so that the kilt fits around the doll's waist Stitch the pleats across the top and one third of the way down the side of each pleat (figure 117).

117
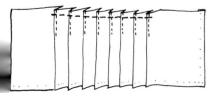

Make a fringe down the unturned edge of the kilt by pulling the warp threads away from the weft threads.
Secure the kilt edge with tiny over stitches (figure 118).

118

Cut a length of bias binding to the same length as the top of the kilt allowing extra for the turning of the ends.
Sew this in place (figure 119).

119
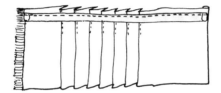

Turn the binding over the top edge of the kilt and slip stitch to the inside of the kilt.
Sew the press-studs to the front cross-over.

Making the jabot
Cut a piece of tape to fit around the doll's neck allowing extra for the back neck fastening.
Cut three pieces of lace each one shorter than the one before.
The width should be double the required finished width. This allows for the gathering.
Place the pieces of lace on top of each other with the longest one on the bottom and the shortest on the top.
Run a gathering thread through all the thicknesses on the top edge.

Pull the gathering thread up so that the jabot is the correct width.
Sew the top edge to the lower half of the tape in the centre (figure 120).

120

Fold the tape down over the top edge of the lace.
Stitch this into place (figure 121).

121

Sew a press-stud to the back fastening.

Making the hat
Cut two semi-circles out of black felt.
Trim the points and sew together (figure 122).

122

Cut an oval shaped gusset to fit between the two semi-circles at the top.
Sew the gusset into place (figure 123).

123

Turn the hat to the right side and decorate it with a band of tartan ribbon around the lower edge.

Making the sporran

Cut out two pieces of white fur to the correct shape and scale (figure 124).

124

With the wrong sides together glue the two sporran pieces together.

Sew a press-stud to the under-side of the flap and to the front of the sporran.

Tie a piece of cord around the waist of the doll allowing it to fall below the belt at the front. Fasten the sporran over this (figure 125).

125

The belt is made from black leather with a cardboard buckle covered in foil.

The shoes are made from black felt and laced at the front.

The socks are made from tartan fabric and held up with elastic garters.

These have flashes sewn to them.

Make the flashes out of ribbon (figure 126).

126

WELSH COSTUME

Measuring

The skirt is measured in the same way as the skirt on page 9 making the skirt full length.

The blouse is the same as the blouse on page 19.

Measure the doll for the shawl making it a triangular shape that will fit around the doll's shoulders.

Materials needed

A length of red woollen fabric
A length of striped cotton fabric
A length of checked fabric
A length of white cotton fabric
Black felt for the hat and shoes
Sewing cotton to match
A piece of cardboard
A press-stud
White trimming lace
Red and white ribbons
Shirring elastic
Rubber solution glue

Making the costume

The skirt

Make this using the red woollen fabric in the same way as the skirt on page 9.

The blouse

Make this using the white cotton fabric in the same way as for the blouse on page 19. Sew the red ribbon around the neck and the cuff edges.

The shawl

This is made from the checked fabric.

Neaten the edges and add a fringe to the two side edges in the same way as on page 64.

The bonnet and the hat

Measure for the brim in the same way as on page 60.

The crown is a cylinder of felt larger at the base than the top, which is closed by a circle of felt (figure 127).

127

The bonnet is made from a semi-circle of white cotton fabric large enough to cover the doll's hair when the fabric is gathered at the front edge and the base.
The curved edge is the face edge.
Turn in and sew a hem around the curved edge.
Make this wide enough to take the elastic.
Trim this edge with the lace (figure 128). This is similar to the bonnet on page 61.

128

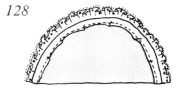

Turn in and sew a similar sized hem along the straight edge.
Thread the two hems with elastic.
Pull up the elastic so that it fits the face edge and the back neck edge of the doll.
Fasten off both ends securely.
Sew two pieces of white ribbon to each of the corners of the bonnet to make the ties under the chin (figure 129).

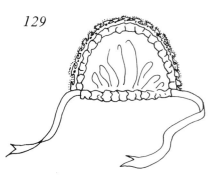

129

The shoes
Make the shoes out of black felt in the same way as on page 62 but trim down to give a shoe with a front flap.
Make two buckles from cardboard and cover them with foil.
Sew these to the front of the shoes (figure 130).

130

A TAHITIAN COSTUME

Materials needed
A skein of natural raffia
Wide tape
Crêpe paper in assorted colours
A press-stud
Rubber-solution glue
Sewing cotton to match
Shirring elastic

Making the skirt
Cut a piece of tape to the same size as the doll's waist measurement adding 1 cm (³⁄₈ in.) for the overlap at the back.
Cut the raffia into lengths which are the same as the finished length of the skirt.

Glue one end of each piece of raffia to the lower half of the tape, leaving 1 cm (³⁄₈ in.) free at the end of the tape (figure 131).

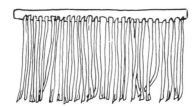

131

Fold the upper half of the tape down over the glued ends of the raffia.
Glue or sew the folded tape together.
Sew a press-stud to the back fastening (figure 132).

132

The flower garland
Cut the crêpe paper into flower shapes (figure 133).

133

Thread these onto a needle threaded with shirring elastic (figure 134).
Alternate the different coloured flowers.

134

When the garland is long enough, tie the ends of the elastic together to form a circle of flowers.
Make a garland for the doll's head in the same way, making the flowers a little smaller.

A RED INDIAN COSTUME

Measuring
Adapt the pattern for the dress on page 13 by omitting the curve for the armholes, this gives a rectangle.
The sleeves are also rectangles but they must have a seam on the top of the arm and shoulder. Remember to allow for the seam allowances.
The length of the tunic is to the middle of the doll's thigh.
The trousers are the same as those on page 22
These should be loose-fitting.

Materials needed
A length of beige sateen curtain-lining
Beige leather off-cuts
A bunch of feathers (a feather duster)
Scarlet, pink and yellow ribbons
An assortment of coloured beads

Rubber-solution glue
Wide brown tape
Fabric paint (optional)

Making the costume
Cut the leather into long thin strips.
The depth of these should be 1 cm ($^3/_8$ in.) wider than the finished depth of the fringe. There must be enough fringing to go down the sides of the trousers and along the top sleeve seam and the lower edge of the tunic.
Make the fringe by cutting the long leather strips from one long edge across to within 1 cm ($^3/_8$ in.) of the opposite long edge (figure 135).

135

With right sides together join the sleeves to the front and back pieces of the tunic (figure 136).

136

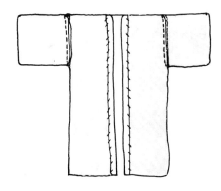

Neaten the centre back edges. With right sides together join the backs to the front at the shoulder and side seams inserting the fringing between the two pieces.

The fringed or cut edge of the leather should face inwards and the uncut edge should be level with the outer edges of the tunic (figure 137).

137

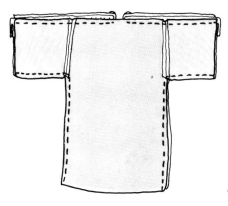

Trim the neck edge into a straight opening.
Neaten this edge (figure 138).

138

Turn up and glue or sew the lower edge into place.
Glue or sew a fringe to the lower edge of the tunic.
Turn up and sew the sleeves edges.
A geometric pattern can be painted or stencilled around the lower edge of the tunic using fabric paint. See page 11.
Make the trousers in the same way as for those on page 22 inserting the fringing in the same way as for the tunic.

The head-dress
Cut a piece of tape to fit around the doll's head and add 1 cm ($^3/_8$ in.).

Join the ends of the band together.
Fold the band in half lengthways (figure 139).

139

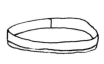

The open edge is the top edge. Cut two lengths of tape for the pieces at the back which hang down.
Fold these in half lengthwise and trim one end diagonally (figure 140).

140

With the diagonal placed on the top edge of the band, glue or sew the two pieces to the headband (figure 141).

141

Glue the feathers between the tape, putting the large feathers at the front of the band (figure 142).

142

Decorate the band with beads. Moccasins can be made out of leather and decorated with beads.

A SPANISH COSTUME

Measuring
The bodice must fit the body closely and come down to the hip-line of the doll.
The bodice pattern can be made by adapting the Simple dress pattern on page 13.
The sleeves are short puffed sleeves.
Measure around the upper arm of the doll and treble this measurement.
Decide on the finished depth of the sleeve and add 2 cm (¾ in.) to this measurement for the seam allowances.
The skirt is circular. The radius of the circle is the required length of the skirt measured from the hip-line, to the doll's feet.
Add 2 cm (¾ in.) to this measurement.

Materials needed
Estimated length of red or turquoise satin or taffeta
Black and red or turquoise lace
Sewing cotton to match
Fuse wire
Three press-studs
Crêpe paper

Making the dress
With right sides together sew the front and backs of the bodice together at the side and shoulder seams (figure 143).

143

Fit the bodice onto the doll. If this does not fit tightly enough make vertical darts at the front and the back (figure 144).

144

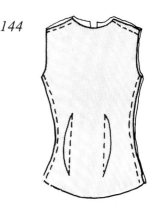

Turn in and sew into place the centre back edges.
Turn the neck edge so that it plunges at the front and the back.
Turn this edge in and sew into place.
Turn in and sew the lower edge of the sleeve.
Run a gathering thread along the upper edge of the sleeve (figure 145).

145

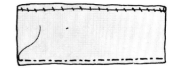

Sew the sleeve into the arm-hole in the same way as on page 27.
Make a slit in the centre of the skirt.
Fit the skirt onto the doll and trim the top edge so that it fits around the doll's hips snugly.
Make a cut for the centre back opening.
Neaten this opening (figure 146).

58

146

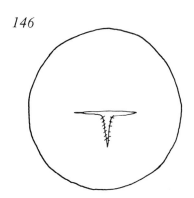

The frills around the skirt are made from lace in alternating colours.
The number of frills depends on the depth of the skirt.
Measure around the skirt where the frill will be sewn and double this measurement.
Cut the lace to the required length.
Join the short ends of the frill together.
Run a gathering thread around one of the long edges of the frill.
Place the frill on the right side of the skirt.
Place the frill in position on the right side of the skirt.
Pull up the gathering thread so that the frill fits around the skirt.
Adjust the gathers.
Sew the frill to the skirt (figure 147).

147

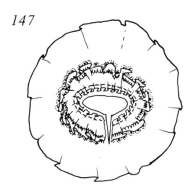

Make the other frills in the same way and sew them to the skirt.
Cut a piece of fuse wire 2 cm (¾ in.) longer than the measurement around the lower edge of the skirt.
Join the ends of the wire together by wrapping one end around the other (figure 148).

148

Turn up the hem of the skirt encasing the wire in the hem. Sew this in place (figure 149).

149

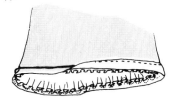

Turn under the lower edge of the bodice.
Place this edge over the hip edge of the skirt matching the centre back openings.

150

Make tucks in the skirt if they are necessary.
Sew the bodice to the skirt (figure 150).
Sew the press-studs to the back opening.
Make a flower for the doll's hair out of crêpe paper.
Cut a length of crêpe paper and cut petal shapes along one long edge.
Roll up the paper and wind thread around the base (figure 151).

151

Open out the petals and stretch the paper to make a full blown rose.
Part the doll's hair in the middle and pull the hair back over the ears to the nape of the neck.
Make a bun in the nape of the neck.
Fasten the flower to the top of the doll's head or behind the ear.

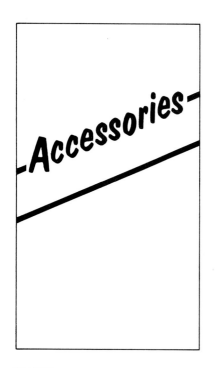

HATS

Measuring

The brim
Using the grid as a guide, measure around the doll's head.

The crown
The measurement A to B, is one quarter of the doll's head measurement.
Add 2 cm (¾ in.) to this measurement.
The measurement C to D, depends on the height of hat required.
Add 2 cm (¾ in.) to this measurement.

Making the paper pattern
It is best to make a preliminary pattern out of newspaper. This can be fitted onto the doll's head and cut and pinned to give a good fit.
Ill-fitting hats have a tendency to fall over the eyes or sit too high on the head.
Using figure 152 as a guide, make the paper pattern as on page 14.
Make the centre hole 1 cm (³⁄₈ in.) smaller than the actual measurement.
Cut a V-shaped notch in the brim to give it a slope (this is not necessary when a flat brim

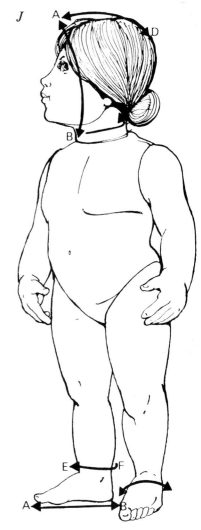

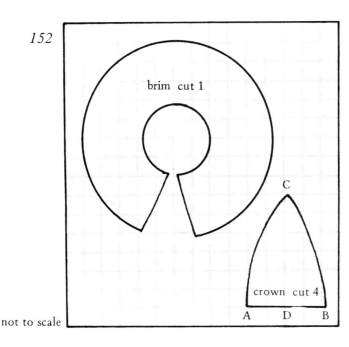

152

brim cut 1

crown cut 4

not to scale

is required, eg for top hats, boaters etc).

Materials needed
The paper pattern
A piece of felt
Sewing cotton to match
Rubber-solution glue (optional)

Making the hat
Pin the pattern to the felt.
Cut out the hat.
Cut V-shaped notches around the inside of the brim, down to the seam line (figure 153).

153

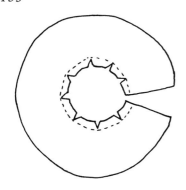

With wrong sides together, sew the four crown pieces together, using a small running stitch (figure 154).

154

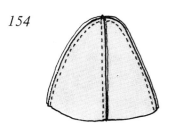

With right sides together, sew the straight ends of the brim. Sew or glue the crown to the brim (figure 155).

155

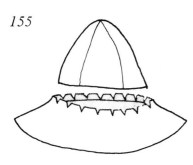

A band of ribbon can be put round the hat to neaten the join.
This basic hat pattern can be easily adapted to make many different styles of hats.

A bonnet

Measuring
Using (figure J) as a guide, measure from point A, to C. Add 2 cm (¾ in.) to this measurement.
Measure from point A, down the side of the doll's face to point B. Add 1 cm (⅜ in.) to this measurement.
Measure from point B, around to the centre back of the neck, point D.
Decide on the size of the circle for the crown. Add 2 cm (¾ in.) to the radius.

Making the paper pattern
Using figure 156 as a guide, make the paper pattern in the same way as on page 14.

156

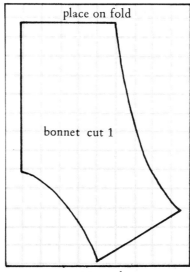

place on fold

bonnet cut 1

not to scale

Materials needed
Estimated length of cotton fabric
A length of ribbon
A length of lace edging
Sewing cotton to match

Making the bonnet
Pin the pattern to the fabric. Cut out the bonnet.
Run a gathering thread along the back edge of the bonnet. With right sides together join the back centre seam (figure 157).

157

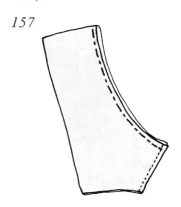

Press in the outer edge of the crown clipping to the seam line where it is necessary.
Pull up the gathers on the bonnet so that it fits around the outer edge of the crown. Adjust the gathers so that they are even.
Sew the crown to the bonnet. Sew a row of lace around the crown.
Fold the ribbon in half lengthwise.
Slip the ribbon over the neck edge of the bonnet, leaving enough free at either end for the ties.
Stitch the ribbon in place (figure 158).

158

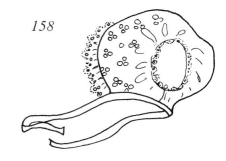

BOOTS

Measuring

The sole
Using figure J as a guide, measure the doll's foot from the toe, point A, to the heel, point B. Add 1 cm (³⁄₈ in.) to this measurement. Measure the width of the foot and add 1 cm (³⁄₈ in.) for the seam allowance.

The sides
Measure around the side of the foot from point A, to B. Add 1 cm (³⁄₈ in.) to this measurement.
Measure from the centre front of the ankle, point E, around the ankle to the centre back of the ankle, point F.
Add 1 cm (³⁄₈ in.) to this measurement.

Making the paper pattern
Using (figure 159) as a guide, make the paper pattern as on page 14.

Materials needed
A piece of felt or leather
Embroidery silk to match
A bodkin or thick needle

Making the boots
Pin the pattern to the fabric. Cut out the boots, (remember to reverse the pattern if the fabric being used has a definite right side).
With wrong sides together, sew the front curve and the back seams using tiny running stitches (figure 160).

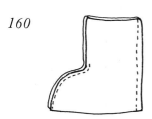
160

Stitch the sole into the base of the boot, matching points A, at the toe and B, at the heel (figure 161).

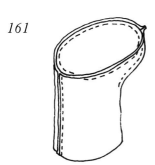
161

Make four holes in each of the sides of the front openings with a bodkin or a large needle. Lace up the boots with plaited embroidery silk or thin strips of leather.
The front of the boots can be decorated with patterns cut from felt and sewn or glued to the front of the boots (figure 162).

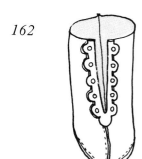
162

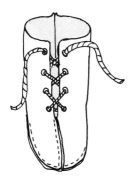

Sandals and shoes
These are measured and made in the same way as the boots, except that they are cut away around the ankle and fastened with a strap and press-stud. Remember to add a little extra to one side of the shoe for the front fastening (figure 163).

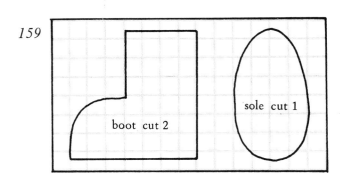
159

boot cut 2

sole cut 1

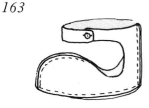
163

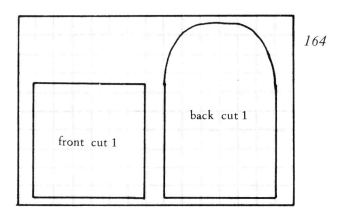

164

back cut 1

front cut 1

BAGS

Materials needed
A piece of felt, leather or canvas
Sewing thread to match
A press-stud
Rubber-solution glue (optional)

Making the paper pattern
Using figure 164 as a guide, make the paper pattern as on page 14.
The front of the bag is square.
The back of the bag is similar but with a flap added.
The sides of the bag are a thin strip, the measurement of which is three times the measurement of one of the sides of the square, plus the required length of the handle.
The depth of this strip determines the depth of the bag.
Remember to allow for the seam allowances on all the pattern pieces.

Making the bag
Pin the paper pattern to the fabric.
Cut out the bag.

165

Sew the short ends of the long strip together (figure 165).
Sew one side of the long strip around three sides of the front of the bag, using small running stitches.
Ease at the corners (figure 166).

166

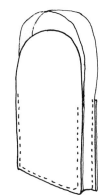

Sew the outer edge of the strip to the back of the bag (figure 167).

167

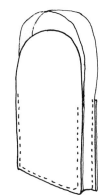

The bag can be turned inside out at this stage or left with the seam as a feature.
Trim the flap and the handle.
Sew a press-stud to the underside of the flap and to the front of the bag.

A BEACH BAG

Making the pattern
The base of the bag is a circle.
The side of the bag is a rectangle the length of which must fit around the outer edge of the base. Add 1 cm (³⁄₈ in.) for the seam allowance.
The depth of the rectangle is the height of the bag, plus 2.5 cm (1 in.).

Materials needed
The paper pattern
A piece of strong cotton fabric
Sewing cotton to match
A length of cord
A piece of cardboard (optional)

Making the bag
Turn in 1.5 cm (⁵⁄₈ in.) on the top edge of the bag. Stitch this in place.
Press under 1 cm (³⁄₈ in.) on the bottom edge of the bag.
With right sides together, sew the side seam of the bag.
Clip around the edge of the base to the seam line.
Sew the bag to the base (figure 168).

168

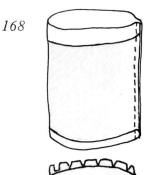

Using a bodkin or a large needle, make holes around the top of the bag.
Thread a piece of cord through the holes and tie the ends together (figure 169).

169

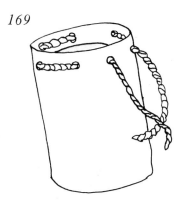

A piece of cardboard the same size as the base of the bag and covered in matching fabric can be put in the base of the bag to give added strength.

SHAWLS AND SCARVES

These can be made of silk, wool or cotton fabric. They vary in size and shape, some being long and thin others triangular or square.
Once the shawl or scarf has been cut out, neaten the edges by turning and hemming.
A fringe on a scarf or shawl makes an attractive edging.
A piece of lampshade trimming can be used for this or you can make the fringe yourself (see below).

MAKING A FRINGE

Materials needed
A ball of 3 or 4 ply wool
A bodkin or a large needle
A piece of cardboard

Making the fringe
Cut the cardboard to the required width of the finished fringe.
Wind the wool round and round the cardboard. Secure the ends of the wool with sticky tape.
Cut the wool along one long edge of the card (figure 170).

170

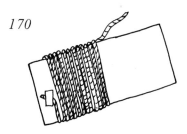

With a bodking or large needle make holes at regular intervals on the edges where the fringe is to be.
Take a few strands of wool by the folded ends.
Push the folded end through one of the holes (figure 171).

171

Bring the cut ends of the wool over the edge of the scarf and pass them through the loop

172

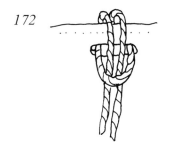

made by the folded ends of the wool (figure 172).
Pull the wool to tighten the knot (figure 173).

173

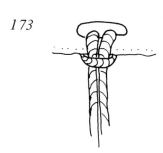

GLOVES

As dolls tend to have small hands and fingers that are joined together it is difficult to make gloves for them — mittens are the answer to this problem.

Making the pattern
Place the doll's hand on a piece of paper and draw around it with a pencil.
This will give you the basic shape.
Remember to allow for the turnings and the fullness for the ease of taking the mitten on and off.

Materials needed
A piece of felt
Sewing cotton to match

Making the mittens
Cut out the mittens allowing for the turnings.
Sew the mittens around the outer edges, leaving the base open (figure 174).

174

Turn inside out.
A piece of shirring elastic can be sewn around the base to help the mittens stay on the doll.
Lace mittens can be made in the same way.

A FAN

Materials needed
Drawing paper
Thin cardboard
Watercolour paint (optional)
Rubber-solution glue
A length of ribbon
Lace and feathers (optional)
A bodkin or a large needle

Making the fan
Cut out an oblong of paper for the main part of the fan.
If you have chosen to paint a design on the fan, now is the time to do it.
Alternatively, the fan can be covered by gluing fabric or lace to the paper.
Fold the fan into pleats (figure 175).

175

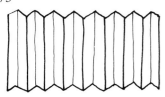

To strengthen the fan cut strips of card the width of the pleats and glue them to the outer pleats (figure 176).

176

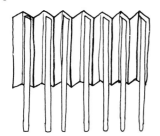

Make a hole through all the pieces of card at the base of the handle.
Thread a piece of ribbon through and fasten it off with a knot (figure 177).

177

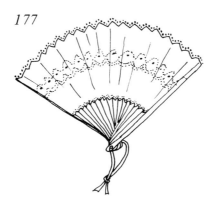

Feathers can be glued to the top edge of the fan to give it an exotic look.

JEWELLERY

It is important to make sure the finished piece of jewellery is in scale with the doll.
Beads can be used from odd earrings, broken necklaces or they can be purchased in packets from craft shops.
Necklaces and bracelets can be made by threading beads onto shirring elastic.
If the beads are too small to thread using a needle, fine fuse wire can be used instead.
Cardboard covered in foil with beads glued to it makes good brooches. A small safety pin sewn to the back makes the clasp.
Sequins glued or sewn to card make pendants and brooches.
Buckles can be made from card and painted or covered in foil.

Jewellery of any kind is not suitable for young children's dolls as they may swallow the beads or hurt themselves on the pins.

SPECTACLES

Fuse wire is used for making glasses as it is easily bent.
Bend the wire to form the frames.
Wrap the wire around a pencil of appropriate thickness to make the eye pieces (figure 178).

178

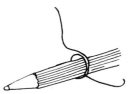

The frames can be painted and a piece of transparent paper glued to the eye pieces to make the lenses.
Coloured transparent paper will make tinted glasses.

AN UMBRELLA

Materials needed
Wire
Bias binding
A piece of cotton fabric
A stick for the handle
Sewing cotton to match
Rubber-solution glue
(optional)

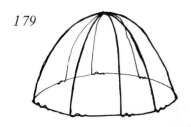

179

Making the umbrella
Using figure 179 as a guide, bend the wire to make the framework of the umbrella. Cover the frame by winding bias binding around the wire. Cut out a circle of fabric large enough to cover the frame.

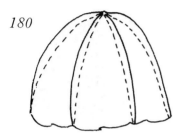

180

Place the fabric over the frame and make darts of equal size down the spokes of the frame (figure 180).

Sew the darts.
Trim any excess fabric from the darts.
With the wrong side against the frame place the cover over the framework and catch stitch into place.
Turn under the raw edge on the lower edge of the umbrella. Sew into place.
Push the stick for the handle through the top of the umbrella so that a short length shows at the top.

181

To prevent the umbrella from falling off the handle, glue a small wooden bead to the handle on either side where it

passes through the fabric at the top (figure 181).
A similar bead can be glued to the base of the stick to form a knob.
To make the umbrella into a parasol a piece of lampshade fringe or edging lace can be glued or sewn around the lower edge of the umbrella. Rows of gathered lace can be glued or sewn to the dart seams.

APRONS

Measuring
A plain ungathered apron with a bib and cross-over straps at the back can be made by measuring the doll in the same way as for the dungarees on page 23.
Substitute a rectangular shape of fabric for the trousers.
A gathered apron is made by adapting the measuring instructions for the skirt with a waistband on page 10.
Make the waistband long enough to tie at the back.
Decide on the finished width of the apron and add half this measurement again and 2 cm (¾ in.) for the allowances.

Materials needed
Estimated length of suitable fabric
Press-studs
Sewing cotton to match
Lace edging
Tape

Making the gathered apron
Cut out the apron
Turn in and sew the lower and side edges of the main piece
Run a gathering thread along the top edge (figure 182).

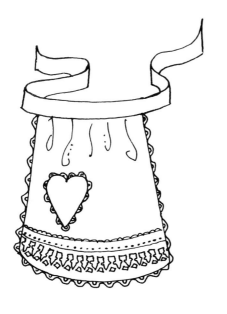

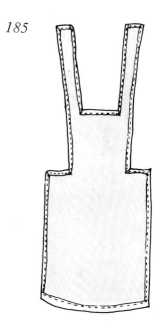

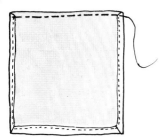

A pocket can be sewn to the apron and the edges trimmed with lace.

186

184

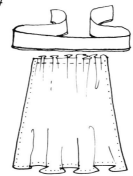

187

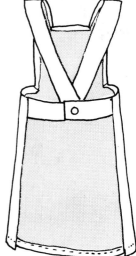

Turn in the seam allowance on all the edges of the waistband. With wrong sides together fold the waistband in half lengthwise (figure 183).

183

Pull up the gathering thread so that the apron is the required width.
Slip the waistband over the gathered edge of the apron.
Sew in place slip stitching the edges of the waistband together (figure 184).

Making the bibbed apron
Cut out the apron.
Turn in the seam allowance on all the edges and sew into place (figure 185).
Fold in the seam allowance on all the edges of the two waistband pieces and sew into place.
With wrong sides together fold the waistband in half lengthwise and slip stitch into place (figure 186).

Sew the waistband pieces to the sides of the apron at the waistline.
Sew press-studs to the ends of the straps and the waistband (figure 187).

This apron can be made into a butcher's apron by using blue and white striped fabric and substituting white striped fabric and making the waistband from tape and the bib held up with a piece of tape attached to the two upper outer corners of the bib.
A carpenter's apron can be similarly made out of white fabric and with a pocket for tools sewn to the front.

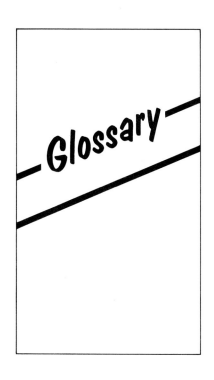

Glossary

Ease	to take away any surplus fabric on a curve or hem by using small pleats or gathers to make the fabric lie flat.
Clip	a small cut made on a curve or into a corner to prevent the fabric from puckering. Make sure not to cut through any stitching.
Turn	to fold the fabric from one side to the other to make a hem.
Hemming	a stitch used to fasten down a folded piece of fabric called a hem.
Gathering thread	a row of stitches which are pulled up to make a length of fabric fit a smaller measurement without cutting.
Nap	the hairy surface of a fabric. The nap should run in the same direction on all the pattern pieces, particularly when using velvet or corduroy.
Grain	the direction in which the lengthwise (warp) and the crosswise (weft) threads of the fabric run
Bias	a true diagonal of the fabric threads. If the crosswise edge of the fabric is placed on the lengthwise edge of the fabric. The folded diagonal is the true bias.
Tacking	a temporary stitch used to hold seams and hems etc. in position until the permanent stitching is in place. A large running stitch is used.
A seam	a permanent line of stitches which holds two pieces of fabric together.
Seam finishes	there are many ways of neatening the raw edges of seams. Pinking shears can be used on fabric which does not fray very badly, or the seam edge can be turned under and sewn down. If you have a swing needle sewing machine a zig-zag finished can be used. Alternatively the edges can be overcast by hand.
Seam allowance	this is the amount of fabric allowed outside the stitching on a seam. This varies in depth depending on the size of the garment being sewn.

Suppliers

Dolls

Dolls can be obtained from specialist toy shops or from department stores. Many of those used for this book were bought second hand from jumble sales.

General

Mary Allen
Turnditch, Derbyshire

Art Needlework Industries
    Limited
7 St Michael's Mansions,
Ship Street, Oxford OX1 3DG

The Campden Needlecraft
    Centre
High Street,
Chipping Campden,
Gloucestershire

de Denne Ltd
159-161 Kenton Road,
Kenton, Harrow, Middlesex

B Francis
4 Glenworth Street,
London NW1

Fresew
97 The Paddocks, Stevenage,
Hertfordshire SG2 9UQ

Louis Grossé Limited
36 Manchester Street,
London W1M 5PE

The Handworkers' Market
8 Fish Hill, Holt, Norfolk

Harrods Limited
London SW1

Ruth John
30 Hunts Pond Road,
Park Gate, Southampton

Levencrafts
54 Church Square,
Guisborough, Cleveland

MacCulloch and Wallis Limited
25-26 Dering Street,
London W1R 0BH

Mace & Nairn
89 Crane Street, Salisbury,
Wiltshire

The Needlecraft Shop
corner Smallgate/Station Road,
Beccles, Suffolk

Christine Riley
53 Barclay Street, Stonehaven,
Kincardineshire, Scotland

Royal School of Needlework
25 Princes Gate,
Kensington SW7 1QE

The Silver Thimble
33 Gay Street, Bath

J Henry Smith Limited
Park Road, Calverton,
Woodborough, nr Nottingham

Mrs Joan L Trickett
110 Marsden Road,
Burnley, Lancashire

Fabrics

Borovick's
16 Berwick Street, London W1
— all types

Bradley Mail Order Textiles
    Limited
Brooke Street Mill, PO Box 24,
Nelson, Lancashire

B Brown Limited
32-33 Greville Street,
London EC1 — felts and
hessians

Dicksons and Company
Dungannon, County Tyrone,
N. Ireland — coloured scrim

Livingstone Textile Company
Bridport, Devon — cheap
fabrics, scrims etc.

N Lockhart and Sons Limited
Linktown Works, Kircaldy,
Scotland KY1 1QH —
evenweaves, scrim

Leathers and PVC

R & A Kohnstamm Limited
Randack Tannery,
Croydon Road, Beckenham,
Kent

John Milner Limited
67 Queen Street, Hitchin,
Hertfordshire — wide variety
of leathers

The Tannery Shop
Gomshall Tanneries,
Queen Street, Gomshall,
Surrey

Venables
Cuxham Road, Watlington,
Oxfordshire — PVC

Suzy Ives	*Making and Dressing a Rag Doll*	B T Batsford
Mary Thomas	*Dictionary of Embroidery Stitches*	Hodder & Stoughton
Walker & Strachan	*Needlework and Cutting Out*	Blackie & Son
Doreen Yarwood	*Outline of English Costume*	B T Batsford

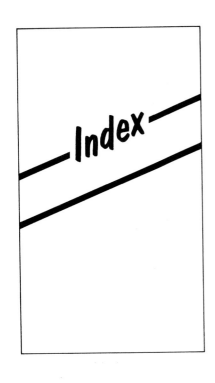

Index